GREAT CAREERS IN
MUSIC

by Brienna Rossiter

FOCUS
READERS.

NAVIGATOR

WWW.FOCUSREADERS.COM

Focus Readers is distributed by North Star Editions:
sales@northstareditions.com | 888-417-0195

Produced for Focus Readers by Red Line Editorial.

Photographs ©: Shutterstock Images, cover, 1, 4–5, 7, 8–9, 11, 12–13, 17, 18–19, 20, 23, 25, 26–27; Reed Saxon/AP Images, 15; Red Line Editorial, 29

Library of Congress Cataloging-in-Publication Data
Names: Rossiter, Brienna, author.
Title: Great careers in music / Brienna Rossiter.
Description: Lake Elmo, MN : Focus Readers, 2022. | Series: Great careers | Includes index. | Audience: Grades 4-6
Identifiers: LCCN 2021001381 (print) | LCCN 2021001382 (ebook) | ISBN 9781644938454 (hardcover) | ISBN 9781644938911 (paperback) | ISBN 9781644939376 (ebook) | ISBN 9781644939796 (pdf)
Subjects: LCSH: Music--Vocational guidance--Juvenile literature.
Classification: LCC ML3795 .R68 2022 (print) | LCC ML3795 (ebook) | DDC 780.23--dc23
LC record available at https://lccn.loc.gov/2021001381
LC ebook record available at https://lccn.loc.gov/2021001382

Printed in the United States of America
Mankato, MN
082021

ABOUT THE AUTHOR

Brienna Rossiter is a writer and editor who lives in Minnesota. She enjoys listening to many kinds of music but especially likes songs that include violins.

TABLE OF CONTENTS

CHAPTER 1

MAKING MUSIC

When people think of careers in music, they often think of pop stars or rappers. But there are many other options. For example, some people perform in groups such as choirs and orchestras. They may give concerts or make recordings. Other people perform background music for plays.

Famous singers such as Lizzo make up a small percentage of the people who have careers in music.

Some people work as session musicians. They play another artist's songs for a concert or recording. Piano players often work as accompanists. They play along with other musicians during lessons, rehearsals, or performances.

Many jobs take place behind the scenes. These jobs may not involve

CONDUCTORS

Choirs, bands, and orchestras often have a conductor. This person leads the musicians as they perform. Conductors help the group play well and stay together. But they do many other tasks, too. Conductors often choose what music the group will work on. They lead rehearsals. They also help plan concerts.

Accompanists are talented performers who can learn music quickly. They can also play in a variety of styles.

performing. But they are key parts of how music is recorded and released. For example, many pop stars hire songwriters.

Few people in music work in just one position. Instead, they often combine several different jobs. As a result, this field is a good fit for people who like variety.

CHAPTER 2

SETTING THE STAGE

At a concert, the audience sees only what happens onstage. But live performances involve many people other than the performer. Some people help with planning. For example, tour managers help artists plan their touring schedules. They also help with **budgets** and payment. Booking agents may

Managers help artists with details such as planning concerts.

be involved as well. They help choose concert **venues**.

Other people work during the performance. Concert technicians set up microphones, **monitors**, and other gear. They fix problems with gear during the concert. And they pack up afterward.

CREATING CAREERS

An artist manager is someone who helps performers create goals and make career decisions. This person also gives artists criticism and advice. Some performers have agents as well. Agents help performers promote their work and find new opportunities. They often help performers communicate with the media, too. This process involves advertising, interviews, and social media.

A sound engineer uses a mixing board to adjust the volume of each instrument during a concert.

Live sound engineers focus on sound quality. They run a sound check before the show. This test makes sure the equipment is working well. The engineers also adjust sound levels and volume during the show. They help create the best sound possible.

CHAPTER 3

IN THE STUDIO

Some artists write and record music on their own. But most artists go to a studio. There, they work with a whole team of people.

The process starts with recording engineers. They convert sound into computer files. To do this, they use equipment such as soundboards

A recording engineer uses many tools to create the best recording possible.

13

and microphones. They choose what equipment to use. And they find the best way to set it up. Engineers often record one part or instrument at a time. Each part is called a track.

A mixing engineer combines these tracks. The layers of sound blend together to create the final song. When mixing, engineers can change the volume of each track. They can also add effects such as reverb.

A producer is often involved with mixing. Producers help find the best sound for a song or album. They help choose what to record and how to mix it. These choices have a big impact

Kanye West is one of the most successful hip-hop producers of all time.

on how the finished song sounds. In fact, producers are sometimes just as important as the singers or musicians. This is especially true in hip-hop. In this **genre**, the producer is often the main artist. Hip-hop producers mix beats and **samples** to create songs.

After music is mixed, it goes to a mastering engineer. This is the last step before the music is released, so the job requires lots of experience. Mastering engineers add the finishing touches. They make sure the music works in a variety

DJs

DJs are people who make and share playlists of songs. Some are hired to play music at events. They often blend songs together or add new beats. Other DJs play songs on radio stations. Many radio DJs host shows. They often focus on a certain genre of music. Some do interviews with musicians or other guests.

Some DJs use vinyl records to create beats.

of formats, such as streaming or vinyl. They also test how the music sounds on different speakers.

Finally, the music is ready to send out into the world. Publicists focus on this step. They help artists gain attention from the media. They make announcements about new music. And they promote the artist's performances.

CHAPTER 4

BEHIND THE SCENES

Many jobs focus on training other musicians. Teaching lessons is a common example. People often teach private lessons at their homes. Others teach at academies. Some even teach lessons online.

Many schools have music teachers. These people teach music classes to

Some people teach piano lessons part-time to earn extra money.

A music teacher helps students play together as a group.

groups of students. Music teachers often lead a band or choir. Several different instruments play together in a band. And choirs involve several different voice parts. So, teachers learn the basics of each instrument or voice part.

In contrast, most private instructors focus on certain instruments or voice parts. Some also teach topics such as music theory or composing.

Composers are people who write music. They write parts for many different instruments. Composers often study music theory. They learn rules and facts about instruments and styles.

Some composers create music on their own. They hope other people will buy their music and play it. Other composers are hired to work on certain projects. For example, many composers create soundtracks for movies, TV shows, and video games.

When working on these projects, composers are often part of a team. They may work with video and sound engineers. These people work on both music and sound effects. In movies, a sound editor is in charge of all the audio. Music editors help plan when music will be used in the film. They make sure

VIDEO GAMES

An audio director is in charge of all the sound in a video game. The director works with the developers and designers to add these sounds and music to the game. The music in a video game is typically connected to certain characters or certain events in the game. Also, the music is often a loop. It repeats over and over until the player begins a new scene.

Music editors ensure that the music matches the images of a movie, TV show, or video game.

the music lines up with what happens on-screen. Music editors work with composers to make any needed changes. Sometimes they write parts of the music, too. When the music is ready, sound editors blend it with dialogue and sound effects.

MUSIC THERAPY

Music therapists use music to help people's mental and physical health. They often focus on helping people deal with stress and pain. Many help treat depression or anxiety. Therapists can work in a variety of places. Hospitals and nursing homes are two examples.

Music therapists have patients create or listen to music. When patients focus on the music, they feel less pain. They feel calmer, too. Music also helps people process emotions. It can help them express things that are hard to talk about.

To become music therapists, people study both music and science. They must get a college degree. They must also pass an exam. Music therapists typically need experience in health care, too. Many work as **interns** or volunteers.

Music can help seniors in nursing homes stay active.

CHAPTER 5

ENTERING THE FIELD

Some people who work in music teach themselves. They figure out how to record and play different sounds. Or they study software for editing music. They get jobs based on **networking** and experience.

Other jobs may require years of lessons and training. People who teach lessons

Nashville, Tennessee, is one of the top cities for country music.

usually study music in college. To teach classes at public schools, people must get a degree in music education.

To go into the business side of music, people learn how to sell and promote music. They learn about running companies and working with the media. They also study **accounting**. Many try to live in cities with **record labels**.

The music field is very competitive, so getting in can be hard. Many people start out as interns. They help teach classes, plan concerts, or do other work. Interns are not always paid. But they build skills and make connections. This experience helps them get jobs later on.

People who work in music often have several roles. And they must develop a variety of skills. Few people become famous. But many find creative ways to do what they love.

CAREER PREP CHECKLIST

Interested in a career in music? Try these steps to get ready.

1 Take lessons to learn a voice part or instrument.

2 Practice performing in concerts, competitions, and recitals.

3 Study music theory and/or composition.

4 Learn to use music production software, such as GarageBand, Logic Pro, or Pro Tools.

5 Learn music notation software, such as Finale.

6 Listen to music from many genres, styles, and locations to learn new trends and ideas.

FOCUS ON
GREAT CAREERS
IN MUSIC

Write your answers on a separate piece of paper.

1. Write a paragraph summarizing how music is recorded in a studio.

2. Which career in music do you think you would enjoy the most? Why?

3. Which person helps an artist gain attention from the media?
   - **A.** publicist
   - **B.** tour manager
   - **C.** booking agent

4. Why do most artists record their music in a studio?
   - **A.** A studio is the only place people can record songs.
   - **B.** Recording in a studio is less expensive than recording at home.
   - **C.** A studio has experts who know how to make the recording sound good.

Answer key on page 32.

GLOSSARY

accounting
A job that involves keeping track of people's money.

budgets
Plans for how money will be used.

genre
A category of music, such as rock, pop, or country.

interns
People who are new to a field and work for little or no pay as a way to gain experience.

monitors
Speakers that face performers so the performers can hear how they sound while they're performing.

networking
Building relationships with other people in hopes of getting jobs or opportunities.

record labels
Companies that help artists put out music.

samples
Small parts of sound recordings that are reused to create parts of other songs.

venues
Places where performances happen.

TO LEARN MORE

BOOKS

Boone, Mary. *Behind-the-Scenes Music Careers.* North Mankato, MN: Capstone Press, 2017.

Harris, Duchess, with Tammy Gagne. *The Birth of Hip-Hop.* Minneapolis: Abdo Publishing, 2020.

Kramer, Barbara. *Lin-Manuel Miranda: Award-Winning Musical Writer.* Minneapolis: Abdo Publishing, 2018.

NOTE TO EDUCATORS

Visit **www.focusreaders.com** to find lesson plans, activities, links, and other resources related to this title.

INDEX

Answer Key: 1. Answers will vary; **2.** Answers will vary; **3.** A; **4.** C